$2.50

The Plenitude We Cry For

A Poem by Sarah Appleton

"I know of no work quite like it, for the unfolding organic **feminine** attentive realization of a natural object, both direct and associative. Rilke entered on things in a similar way but not at this length."

John Berryman

The Plenitude We Cry For

The Plenitude We Cry For

SARAH APPLETON

1972

DOUBLEDAY & COMPANY, INC.

GARDEN CITY, NEW YORK

Library of Congress Catalog Card Number 72–76113
Copyright © 1972 by Sarah Appleton
All Rights Reserved
Printed in the United States of America
First Edition

The Plenitude We Cry For

This is the record of one season's growth of a horse chestnut tree in 1964 at Northampton, Massachusetts. The tree is small, with a double trunk, and it stands in front of a grey frame house, which faces east and the morning sun. I viewed the tree from my writing table at a second-story window and also standing on the ground next to the tree, where I could touch the branches. After the tree flowered, I cut off one flower from a cluster, placing it with water in a porcelain dish in front of my notebook. In summer I brought a leaf and nut upstairs to my table to dissect them.

The record was written out of bareness, from a completely new beginning. It tells of a double life: that of the tree with the earth, sunlight, rain and wind and living creatures around it and that of myself interpreting with the tree's life. The form is a series of notes imitating the stages of the tree's growth: reflective, concentrated and elliptical, exploding, enumerative, suspending, dispersing, in summer spare and mechanical. The ugly or harsh sounds as well as flat statements are part of the economy of the tree.

The tree is the center. Trusting myself to the tree, I placed no restrictions on the range of forms embodied in the tree's growth—human and intelligent, animal, temporal, mathematical, musical, color, rhetorical, cosmic, sacrificial. The restrictions that exist are those periods of time when I was not present to observe and the limitations of my power to interpret. These create the intervals between the notes.

Part One

I

Today   my tree stands
bare, branch tops like young horned deer
velvet grey
winter horned

Today
my body tells far more—the sap lives here

first red or pale yellow green, light will first fill
skin and fiber then thrust to bud. I feel the tapping
in my stream—O body against time, body against air
body in shift to dust, against each new spring

II

Spring rain

Horns have thickened
each tip sprouts out a felted knob
like a preacher thrust into his pulpit—see
eleven preachers
on a preacher candelabra
their small bodies stiff with joy

III

God demands that poetry should burn

This thought came from spring rain
that now silts down
casting a white ground—

IV

Each branch blushes like a human face
Now what was grey glows

Our faces shift by the heart's pulse,
these burn by deeper sun

V

They are slow to turn; so that we, watching
can rest in time

VI

For a month this still tree has transformed
from stone, to felt horn, to limb.
In light now white against my window
or in slow rain it grows new stiff arms.

What shall it change in time—
I live other pressures, as whirling
from place to place, as suffering, weak
fears, joys, as unending forming
to God's fire.

Black and golden, hung now with lights
of rain, what mystery
shall we draw—

VII

Suddenly, as if roof sways the sky moves
on pilaster trees writhing like weeds under waves
clouds roll in swells

swooping, a bird grips the tree and holds

the branch sways

VIII

Can we be more beautiful than these
branch tips, lace to sky
swaying like sea fans,
the fret work of blowing trees?

Our eyes are hooded to our action's splendor.

Unlike trees
our form is light in light
or lacking, is blind white.

IX

The sun burns

light diffused through earth's air
to my window frame
casting a shadow like bars
on curtain folds, my books, paper, hands

Here as in underwater shadows
my heart is shaded bemused
wandering with time

Yet I breathe the invisible fire in which the sun burns

X

I took one branch down
to find the secret form
and saw
form no canvas could hold
heart form, growing up and out from the pit as if
I must stand in God's view to look down and in
rough blown, shingle form, thumbnails or husks
beating up—all is horn and the heart is the nut.

Each twig, thumb thick, turns to hard flame, flame cased in flame
husk
but each twig does not all bud; dry flames seal growth angles
each smooth limb holds dry horn skin. The brown smooth as amber
stone
bears pale flame
shadows of the nut's form.

Part Two

XI

As rock to earth: to seed to bud;
growth to birth; birth to growth—
no dead thing is. Time=to transform.

In this tree, through five suns, simply, a new cosmos is born
impossible to call it merely "form," or
imitation of form.
To it we must be humble
knowing no forms ever, although we live celestial form
and this, serves us—
humble to it, as to one who deeply loves us
so deeply loving that he is hidden to us,
as all power lies hidden from which we feed,
as around our heart, seeming so freely beating,
we beat inside the heart of light.

XII

The shell from shell from shell has blown
pushed up two curled hands like furled wings
knobs touching knobs, in shadow green and veined,
in aura white and sticky as from the womb
                rough thought like the bark
the bud grows from the arms of four husks
starts where the flat scars knob and grow
the still flat scars lined with little nails,
and husks up, evolving in turns like a spiral
/brown, to green with brown tips/
then pushed apart by the bulk of the leaf
the lower husk falls back like a lip, the whole hitching up
in alternate stairs of growth

XIII

Today the tree dreams
of what it shall be, no dream in the mind
as we dream, but that flesh forms.
The buds thrust in groups, whitebrown green
by threes and not threes, alternate and not
hitch up each limb as flying drops or
heavy swans' wings opening. Too heavy to be fire.
They are weighty prophets of that second stage
after the flowers shed down, leave
green leaves and white embryos of nut.

XIV

two suns   :

the dream explodes
        tatters of green
        swirls into nests and clusters

creatures spring out of the branches
        struggle to air
        out of the limbs flutter up, stretch cone-like necks—
        shake wings out

birds of paradise, slanting, tails asplash
        fish leaping from spray
        jet blasts—phoenixes

by transformations   :   tree from within seeks new element
            beyond and up, to a point of tension

you can see the tree is thinking all over   That bud adumbrates
what that shall be, who remembers what that bud was once,
speaks its own seed to its last form—which I cannot see ahead
except as now the tree top is horned with cones above harpies' wings
these cones to flowers as nut is to bud, and bud to these cones

XV

From bud, to curled hands, back to back: form furled from within
furl, out around, open to such splay that seven leaves fall back
from each hand to hang down, like clothes in the wind, revealed:
to second cluster, thrust between the first gauze stems up around,
to flower open then fall back and down, like the first, heart and
inner core drawn up to sun to rust and glow: to this third, more
fine, more simplified mirror pair of only five—the whole is one, to
four husks, to seven upon seven leaves hung alternate, to five, like
stars—

stasis in design: so that suddenly form rests can be seen as an image
of the tree itself

A concentration within as if brooding new birth

(numbers are to be sounded)

Or

1 The left bud draws back like a paw
   its heart a creased fan into which the opposite furls
2 These paws splay out into two pointed fans
   held in precise spatial form
   by a power that proportions space entire—
   within, without, in relation to: visible, invisible
   in essence all modes of knowing—past, present and future—
   as power of music
3 This secret: to multiply and to reveal; and to concentrate and
                                              to recall;
   the whole always turning, unfolds into seven leaves
   the mirror of seven leaves opposite;
   each seven divided by a vein, itself a mirror to itself,
   stiff, pointed lucent leaves, stretching from lighter veins
4 Power upon power: at alternate angle, as these new leaves
   are alternate angled to the longer husks,
   the heart thrusts a second cluster dividing up and out
   while the first has opened back upon itself
   fallen into inverse memory of itself in relation to its stem,
   holds there, the light gauze turned red golden by the sun
   supreme inner gift of veins and heart to light
5 While Three through the furze of gauze is thrusting again
   alternate angle to Two, which is flying up and folding back
   as One has done, who hangs like skirts or drooping wings
   as Three unfurled brings stasis to the form:
   signed and interpreted by this third fan of five leaves
   symmetrical to its stem as seven repeated seven was, only five—
   while Two hangs drooping as skirts or drying wings,
   heart rust and gold gauze to sun in inverse memory to the stem
   of how it was born by the memory of the birth of One:
   And miracle—after the rise and fall of the leaves to themselves,
                                              opening

and reflecting, against their opposing pairs, like a music of
                                        mirrors—
a fourth wave draws; a golden sound from the sun hums through
                                        their veins
elevates ascends the lucent wings to the air
so that the whole tree flashes and plays with green fire
itself shading and revealing leaf by leaf, and lifts
like the skirts of dancers

6   Two small green claws emerge from the center
like ribbed shrimps upside down
pointed tips (or tails) uncurl
to make

7

Part Three

XVI

They spring like Christmas tree candles, hierarchies of them
at first like new budding trees from within older leaves
which now hang and sway like flat-topped billows
underneath fan upon fan suspended by air and sun

They push out from the tight throats of the limbs
or as child thrusts out between the mother's spread legs
these flowers burst from the inner thrust that split
the first bud, burst pair upon pair from the bud's
heart adumbrate of flame, amber and nailed nut.

XVII

By one flower the whole tree takes new form.

Thrust up within the same fine gauze the flower's heads
curl; pale, blurred as if held in a womb,
buds all concentrate within, within gathering to be born
and not to the same time, but one by one—as pink tongues
or feet spilling from within, the inner heart falls open

pours down loosening as lips into white skirts
so that as if one whole side were caught in lights,
the flower tree floods, hollows into the living air
palpable fire.

XVIII

Each leaf fan has perfected. The seven blades rise
symmetrical to themselves above their rust-haired stems,
playing the wind as if floating on water, held by the sun
flat to the bowl of the sky—the eunuch ones;
those fertile soar like heavy-skirted dancers
from the mind of the tree which breathes fire and air.

XIX

To the Element of Flower

Green knob: inward bent, as a head bows—
   splays of these
   cast over the center stem thrusting—
Loosens: spills pink slippers down
   seven fall, from the fluted lips blown wide

From the knob as an arched hand: flower is thrown to air—
   furls back into four petals
   seven white stalks drop down
   pink slippers shed from rust red drops
   which, lightened, flare up to suspend

Recalls the two possibilities of a wave:
   which flowing, may crash against new element and
   as these petals, furl, burst back high upon itself;
   or unbound, roll upon roll in recollection and self-perpetuation
   as these stalks, rise up and collect, like a whip, their first fall's
                                   curve

Both. This flower is also the echo of the unfolding of leaf
   from the leaf: the leaf wave
   which fell back upon itself,
   fell back up to the sky's face,
   falls back from the flower's blaze

And the culmination of the substance of the tree
   which was white:
   the first gauze womb around bud
   is the thin hood over these flowers' heads,

Now is burst in the revelation of its music to the air

Has brought this tree to the elements of air and fire
   as the wind plays the flower to the light
   the flower bursts the wind into fire
   as light is the interpretation of the flower

For, see, these clusters' music is color!
   palest at top pure white flower
   then cast to yellow like the glow of butter
   deeper back to the stem the hearts are pink

The surface of the cluster flies, spiked with red tipped thorns

And even the flowers' stem bears new white shadows of the thorns.

XX

(To see the flower
is to cut it from the cluster.
Falls, bounces; holds:
to put it to the light, dissect.

*

Pod tips salmon
split by body of the stem,
shadow of the inner nut,
perhaps dictate the whole thought.

Die anyway=Butter yellow to crimson.
What is it? not the sun has translated,
no sap has—lying in ½ inch of water, on porcelain
against gold thread of wheat; has furled over
like a creature flailing seven rust pods
back under lucent water, breathing water.

Yellow to red/detached from life blood=echo
of change in the tree that is turning

Death is

absolute mutation: yellow/red

timed to the red pods' thrust
heaving the body down
and to expansion from the heart: like bursting sheaves
barrel staves, swelling outswelling to twist to the petals falling

dispersion, dispersed, pollen sifting: invisible thrust to invisible
petal and pods falling

*

The Key, the tone, the mortal tune is red
has been red

as the first bud husks first tuned like shells the flow of leaves
from which flowers were tuned and held, curled and dried
like beetle shards, red
touched, they crumbled down—
as I cut this flower, which when it first fell, bounced, held,
should I touch now would shatter

as the gauze of these tiger mouths—

having been the substance of the womb of the leaves' aura for eyes
and sticky touch by sun burned, red)

XXI

Yellow bees wax, or ivory filigree; flower recalls butter,
rocks, precious ambergris, and smooth horn—to this
the heavy heavy bees, black burs, like cumbrous spiders
fall and hang
sensing the living from the dead—fall upon the yellow open hearts
to copulate
the rest falls as ashes, dry foam, tree dust
where bee never falls; who is held to the flower's live hold
against its pale green shell

*

comes down, moving to the wind, flower moving
moves on the flower, thrusting under like a bell

XXII

Sterility: instead of splits of three leaves to flower's four petals
and tensile of seven pods
is fives, and two stub end claws

is for the first time defined by the flowers drawing bees,

is to do with how the world beyond the tree is drawn and draws,
no longer is bursting to be born, but bears itself and sleeps to
       maintain a dead balance

            *

from the outside—clouds, swallows, winds
rain and sun,

lying wide to these as bodies to the air corrode,

has relaxed, will grow bland to lie unobserved in summer

XXIII

The flowers' age is air—see the moment whole,
    each petal strung, free
    trunked, like a cluster of trees;
    intricate wombs of the air

released, overcome, dispersed
here by what is unfallen after entire fall, and each petal's;
here couched, hard whole, bristling minute horned
tree substance of nut
            —adumbrated, haloed by the flower
              as its interpretation
              as its mortal rhetoric
        as succulent delusion for the bees (sent by their other literal
                                          lives)

    as superflux and camouflage

XXIV

Rhetoric

A law:

      that of profusion of flowers, a profusion
scatter

have flamed, borne light and air within their petals
as one element of the total flower's concentration and reflection
of the trees-within-the-leaf reflection of the tree—these as
wild and scattered swirls around the stem:
                        having
curled, spilled, reflexed up, flared
in white translucence, to the beat of the changes of its heart's
color—white pure, to wax-like yellow, to red opposing rust re-
flected red—
tensed: a total rhythmic house that radiates like a bur—

have fallen
all over the ground under the tree in a waste of beauty:

That beauty is not the secret of energy,
if we have beauty;
but the secret of chance—drawing admiration for us
and a sense of mortality, if we see—
profuse so that the casual bee and the wind can fall anywhere
                                    constantly

XXV

(There shall be four days of waste: time will pass blind
to what might be seen—being worked within like spider
gestates, or hard pearl: broken to time as a bent lute
hooded as sewn hawk's eyes—Miraculous transformations
of eternal plenitude we cry for, for all the generations' articulate
sacrifices—this agony; as a mother's birth agony hidden,
as the father's malehood sacrificed, as the
            eunuch's particular splendor
unaccepted—to be split as a rock by silence
yet to breathe)

XXVI

To look at the tree is not to be distracted in mortality
although the watcher fears the wind's tearing off the last flowers
and the tree's turning invisible and dull—is to look at the tree:
is to look at the *tree:*
is now to be unable to speak of these new white life-giving burs
is not to start from the flower; but is, to go back, lay your head
against the trunk, to embrace what feels, to suffer weight—is
to prophesy so far forward to the time these spines solidify
where now they are babies milk-toothed, like marrow bone:
is to strike the dominant of the tree: here, more than
deep in the roots; here, more than in the leaves' crotch;
here, more than any thought you can remember thinking:
                    concentrate.

Part Four

XXVII

With a knife I split the stem of the leaf
and cut crossways, and with my nails I slit back green skin.
I watched the juices collect at the joint of the stem.
I severed the center peeling out the five reins of life
so that I could palpably know the law to this tree.
From the flat leaf I deduced the past motion of the leaf bud.

And while I studied this with a voracious appetite
for the tangible, the summer has come, has set dryness
in my mouth and set my music into dryness

and I have been made into a strange lute
singing a measure that may be cut off.

XXVIII

The first mystery of the bur (secretes drops of light, frail silk
as if catching tiny threads of wind, or hair around horns
to lure what creature? Soot specks? Fine banners,
glints from the wind) is living/dead; light/palpable
growing/unmoving—couched like a sea urchin.

XXIX

To see, bur must be turned. Two white lines
dictate a path in the indiscriminate sea of thorns.

To see=to slice and to destroy—active energy
from us, its master: sacrifice to our thoughts' hunger
according to that command "All things subdue"
as vases of living flowers cut, and those chosen souls
enclosed, singing their hearts out, sacrifice

XXX

These burs splayed on spines are models of atoms
irregular to man's geometry: adumbrate swirling fire,
planets' whirling—infinitely slow,

the out-whirling of the burs on the spines
the in-volving of the bulb within the bur
simultaneous, exactly as the spheres of Paradise
and planet epicycles, enclose miraculous fragility
of infinity: genius

XXXI

The tree cosmos grows Ptolemaic because
it is fixed on this earth. The music is sent from the earth
shocking up the central trunk, out along the branches
to the leaf clusters to snap into flowers. Like water in buckets
ours by their inner swirl burst to fly off, and they will.

*

They mirror what our fine instruments tell us:
that we habit our bodies whirling away as fast as they can
from our view in God's infinitely everywhere

XXXII

and also the skeleton of a man
balancing, balancing; the bones of the juggler
with weighted hands flung out, compelled
compelled to play gravity's game

yet fixed
by *this* incarnation, by slow growing

           *

(Mind flashes around like lightning refuses
to be slow

which the patience of charity
demands, the flame of charity
for the slow)

XXXIII

Carved out. Trunk and branch stiff
leaves seem flutters, water splashes, severed from the fact
of trunk shagging, of branch, packed scar upon scar
from stem upon stem—succulence has drifted.

Carved out, bone-like—limbs shine hard, set
the nuts. Element:rock. Air=reflected rock.
Strike that rock, sound it. Set bone of ear flat to it.
Draw salt, diamond.

(The limits=hope and what drew and cast the bees,
the changing winds like my feeble will waves far
from any sure body or hope of this)

XXXIV

summer is like winter waits only the life
is visibly stilled not invisibly tense the heart's place
easier not wrenched by expectation that exceeds
but sleep alive as the effect of all constancy
sleeps like the sea so sleeps the dream

XXXV

fierce wind rips in: insects, dust
wearing out toughness to the measure of endurance

XXXVI

Life is drawn out by the incubating nut
as if strings were pulled taut in cloth
the leaves stiffen up, economy to life

*

The tree's beauty
now=sacrifice for the cultivation of the nut.
The whole heavy body, limbs, leaves upon leaves
has suppressed its history into its substance—
no prophecy, no memory—has set us free to float
in itself, with it, wave over wave, stilled,
so that our body and limbs rise loose in the water;
is the quality of this time, to be sunk into the eye of eternity.
I suppose I am thinking of the tension of the leaves
floating to the waves of the sun, weathering over their vulnerability

SUMMARY

The tree	same dry trunk—it must grow unseen: now ants
	eat the heart so that it bursts out sweet
The branches	as Daphne, between the first and second
	pair of leaf stems have petrified brown
	skin bears freckle marks from reins' ends
	will bear four flame shadows when stem falls
The leaves	strength less than wind are sucked by sun
	insects feed on them, by drought are drawn down
The organs	still intricate significant at joint of flower;
	or where I saw claws where was no flower
	is hard armored bud; where flower was
	two are ready to bifork next year's bud
Time	By this fact summer contains next spring
	begins frozen by intense heat long
	before any cold (when we will attend
	because the distracting green has fallen)
	clasps them in what shall be second ice;
	intimates that birth of spring as each leaf
	of this tree has been by multiplication, is heat
	upon cold which by disbalance loosens
	these infinite fantasies and fulfillments
Duplicity	Attention has been withdrawn from the leaves
	the leaves and nuts have been sacrificed
	the juices dawn out of the stems and down
	so that leaves hang to the whole tree detached

The flower   The stem top points like a snail's horn
exactly one half inch above the first nut stem
choked—nuts hang over the relaxed leaves
The nuts   Fate is translated to law of mechanics:
The power fed by juice to stem bends
under increased weight fed by juice to nut
until the stem snaps and launches the nut;
this law figures palpably the tree's past:
first the stem swells full of the juices,
the nut is tiny bud; then flower falls as
the nut swells and the stem dries until
heavy with involutions the nut plummets;
the law is in direct ratio to the balance
of sun and rain the test of which is the wind

Double Future

Consistent to the dream of itself in the mirror
this tree concentrates into two destinies:
as the nuts grow heavy within to detach
and carry off the colony of a second tree
new hard-horned buds set, single by the sterile
cluster or double by the stem of fertile cluster

By palpable analogy to the flower

in final movement of the wave the nut
has fallen down and hangs ready to break off,
the nut will float in earth on its thorns
then in generation of the tree repeat
as flower grown into the medium of stone—
as the inverse of the flower's flair, hard to air
where the flower's petal was devoured; as the
obverse of the flower a liquid amber
at the center as the flower bore its honey;
organed as the flower having spilled down
salmon slippers to the air and bee,
red tipped roots will burst and tap
the thicker medium of the solid earth,
and as reverse mirror of the flower,
not spilling then recoiling to its face
shall rather shove their house to the air upon its feet

Horse Chestnut Tree Forms

(The leaves)

The Mirror   The mirror is a principle of form in motion as well as stasis (For example, the opposite pairing of leaves; the opposite alternating multiplication of pairs).

The Wave   The wave is the type of motion. In appearance the leaf opens like a topped crest of a wave

and a swirl or spiral (How does a wave open/re gravity, re its continuous motion—the wave motion in this tree is a law of growth. What is the relationship of the forms of growth to gravity?).

The Mirror and Wave Together   As the leaf pair unfolds: first in two mirror relations—it opens until the inner heart of each leaf fan replaces the position of the bud's tip as the uppermost point and until the inside becomes outside, as the leaflets hang down, limp, enclosing the stem in a vague recollection of the bud enclosing; then the leaves of each pair rise up again, stiffening, as if drawn up by the sun, into its two opposing fan shapes. In what way is space a part of the *power* of the form? The leaves seem to be tuned to it, the air solid by it.

This leaf pair's unfolding is reproduced by a *second* pair of leaves unfolding in alternating balance to the first pair and at a level higher.

The *third* pair reveals the crucial development; again unfolding in alternating mirror and balance to the second, but with a profound difference. It is an analogous mirroring rather than an exact reflection (As, looking back, it appears all the mirrorings have been).

Whereas the first two pairs were each made up of seven leaflets, the third pair may reveal *three* leaflets only, or it may reveal *five* only. If it reveals five, it will be sterile of flowers, and at the crotch of the stem and the trunk of the leaf cluster to fulfill the law of seven, it will produce two stubby claw-like trunks—abortive.

If it reveals three leaflets, the law of seven in the lower leaves will be fulfilled for the third pair of leaves by the complementary four petals of the flower.

Number What exactly is this variation within seven, the relationship of the three leaflets on the third fan pair to the next projection of four petals of the flower? It is a *numerical analogy* or mirror of the first two (alternatingly poised) pairs of fans, including a substantial change: that of leaf to petal—dividing the number seven into three and four. The number is the overarching law, inclusive; binding the flower into a unit with the last pair of leaves. Seven is the inclusive numerical law of the tree and enables us to *see* the tree's development by difference to itself, yet within itself.

But also, the four-petaled flower unfolds from a *five* petaled sepal which is like a shell, an echo of the sterile *five*-bladed fans not to bloom or grow further. Does this make the following numerical relationships?

3 leaves to 4 petals=7   to

2 elements (leaves and petals)   to five petaled sepal=7?

What is the *power* of number that is involved in growth?

The tree develops by *multiplication* and *revelation*, by a *mirror* and *wave* principle.

*

Interpretation within the Tree: History and Prophecy

All this can be *read* in the branches of the tree, by which the number of the later years of growth can be read.

There are flame-shaped *scars* (areas of texture change, visually analogous to those on the nut) on the branches, left by the blade of leaf falling later—the branches *pack* these scars (multiplication), one on top of the other, recording what has grown.

Below each scar packing is a circle of wrinkles (The marks, I think, of the first stipule burst by the first bud of the first pair of leaves because the stipule embraced the entire branch surface).

Each scar has *four* possible readings (That is, *ideally*—one of the miracles of the tree is also its individuality and irregularity, which can be read here as well. The life is also *exceptions* to the principles. As in the handling by the poet of traditional meters, the principles of form seem to be ideal tension and force behind the concrete existence of the tree which is open to events beyond and outside the ideal law within the tree—content of soil and air, weather, disease, rending by living moving creatures, and unnamable events).

First is the record of the leaf's own fertility or sterility in producing flowers. Marking the outer edge of the lower part of the blaze are nail-like knobs, seven of them— or on what must have been the sterile stems, five. These record what the leaf produced, flowers or air. If the sterile stem of a leaf fan is torn off, it will show five threads ruptured, as if reins guided from somewhere, at some point (not here—perhaps in the flower, later) to sterility.

There is another variation which has two possibilities, the record of the leaf's sterility or fertility in producing branches and leaves. At the top of some of the scars is another, larger knob. This is the place where the new bud has come and failed. I have not looked to see at what angle in relationship to the others' scars the bud comes.

The branches and leaves of a cluster without flowers are packed more tightly on each other; the branches and leaves of the clusters which bear flowers *grow* between the alternating pairs. Strength and size has been given to them by bearing the flower.

*

(The Flower)

The topmost pair of *three*-leaved fans, completed by the *four* petals supported by the *five*-shelled sepal has *seven* pollen-bearing stamen.

It opens exactly analogous, in a mirror reflection (at a later time; in this way it is a recollection), of the *mirror-wave* motion of the leaf fans—but embodies *two* developments of the wave instead of one.

The first, the opening of the four petals, is like a wave that meets the resistance of the wind and breaks into foam, is penetrated by light and air. The buds begin arched down like the wrist arching with a closed hand. Stamen, tipped by slippers of pollen, spill down and out of the mouth of the flower (or the relaxing fingers) as the petals draw up and back (as the leaves did). Then the petals suspend open.

The second wave motion, simultaneous with the folding back of the petals, occurring in the length of the stamen, is a wave uninterrupted. After spilling down in an arch, the stamen retain the arch, as a whip does in the air; then, rearing up again, to suspend, they oppose the face of the suspended petals. For a time both the stamen and petals are held tense in their double possibility of the wave, giving a dimension to the air.

The timing of the flower is by color. The petals as they first unfurl, as the leaves did, show white hearts. As the flowers develop and the stamen rear back up to the face of the petals, the hearts have become *yellow*. At this time the bees come.

By the time the heart turns *red*, the inner tension of the whole flower has loosened. It flares apart from itself from within, until each petal and each stamen is poised on a separate stem of support, the whole like a lantern to the air. The bees never touch the flowers as the flowers achieve their red hearts. The wind blows the flowers apart and their elements scatter.

As there are sterile and fertile leaves, so there are two kinds of flowers—sterile and fertile. I have described the sterile flowers—which are profuse.

The fertile flower is marked by an eighth, white feeler which protrudes from the lip of the bud to mark the first point of the flower's unfolding and which projects all during the motion of the wave. The bee inserts himself to this, resting his feet on the rust slippers of the stamen.

The fertile flower bears a *formal* relation to the sterile flower which has been a *mirror* of the fertile flower. The fertile flower is to the sterile as a *substance* and a *fulfillment* is to its *adumbration*.

What has forced the sterile flower open from within to fall and scatter is the power and concentration within the petals of the fertile flower—the new nut, which swells at the base of the white feeler: from which the petals which have turned red at the heart fall away —revealing the hard-greenwhite bur.

*

Mirrors within the Whole

The flower cluster is made of a small white trunk which grows from the top crotch left by the third leaf-pair of three leaflets.

It is more a mirror of the whole *tree*'s growth than of the growth of the leaf clusters which worked in exactness of opposition to each other's angle of growth.

As do the whole tree's branches, so the flower clusters reflect the wave. The flower's branches develop in a swirling circular relation to the central trunk, mounting to the top, each branch in turn developing clusters of buds, not determined either, as far as I can see, by regular angles.

Each individual leaflet of a fan of seven leaflets is a *two dimensional reflection* of the laws of the leaf cluster's growth.

As I remember, in the first opening of the leaf, the leaflet—as well as mirroring its opposite in the cluster—mirrors itself—the right side mirrors the left—and after falling back up to be suspended by the sun (or whatever gives the leaf its tension to splay out as a fan), the individual leaflet (on the upper limbs of the tree mostly) folds back, towards itself—like a razor clam closes—and holds, like a long trough.

The stem and veins of an individual leaflet show a new proportion to the growth of the leaf cluster, embodying the *mirror* and *wave* by means of a *flat medium.*

The veins alternately oppose each other across the central stem, but staggered in alternating parallel positions—not equi-spaced, but the right veins spaced closer to those lower, sometimes touching the lower.

I would say, without knowledge, that this unequi-spaced alternation is the reflection and cause of the circular swirl of the unfolding: that when the leaf was curled in the bud, the opposite veins might have touched, having the potentiality of different rates of separation as the stem grew—the fact that the right viens are closer to the left-lower veins than to the right veins above perhaps indicates that the swirl of the unfolding went in clockwise motion.

The *veins within the leaves* (again in adumbration of the tree) have very pure lines that can be read. The central trunk is straight; the veins from it flow straight, parallel, and there is no involvement until they approach the flame-like teeth of the leaf's edge. Near the edge the parallel veins throw out *curving* branches. These curves are directly analogous to the position of the left veins higher than the alternating right. The curving branches reach up to the leaf's edge. The reach of the veins on either side of the stem is in mirror-relation to the other, reaching up from the *lower* side, if the point of view is the fan's center, reaching down from the upper side, if the view is from the trunk of the tree.

Color as the Measure of Time

Color is the element of life and death: white green is the inner life substance. It forms the initial womb-like gauze around the buds of both the leaves and the flowers. The leaves and the flowers at the early stages appear white-green, as are the veins of the leaf.

There is a *mirror reflection of white and green* in relationship to *outer and inner*, seen in the color relation of the stem of the leaf to the unfolded leaflet. The unfolded leaflet's trunk and veins are whitish, and as they expand to the leaflet's edge, they grow more and more translucent, while the color within the stem, which is enclosed in a fine skin the shade of the leaf's central vein, is a whitish pulp lying around the central reins of fertility and sterility which are green.

Red is the element of death. The gauze from the leaves after their unfolding clings at the heart of the fan, and the sun in a day burns it a rust red. The pod of the leaf, sticky, falls back and dries into a rust red. The time of the diffusion of the flower by the air is paced by a change to red—this red is not rust, but a medieval "purple" red.

Dusty brown-grey seems to be the color of solidity and continuity. The fertile green leaf trunks of the clusters gradually dry and harden to tree branch brown.

"I have used THE PLENITUDE WE CRY FOR in manuscript to demonstrate to students certain possibilities of attention and the discovery of precise language that can emerge from such attention. It seems to me a remarkable piece of work, in which something of the objectivity of Francis Ponge and the empathic relation to *things* of Rilke are conjoined: i.e., it embodies some of what can be learned from each, and does so in a fresh, personal, unrhetorical way. The rhetoric, that is, is truly the *tree's* rhetoric, not the writer's."   *Denise Levertov*

"This is one of the great and desperate poems of the feminine, the feminine trying to live."   *George Oppen*

"I know no other long poem like this—mysterious, speeding up and growing more complex as it goes along, seeking 'with a voracious appetite for the tangible' through observations of a tree's growth to learn what it means to be human, woman, to bear, to be laid waste, to be transformed within earthly time."   *Jane Cooper*

"The tree and the woman poet who, with the precision of a botanist, observes the tree are identified with life's processes of transformation and perpetuation as the tree becomes a metaphor of life itself. . . . A painstaking explanation of her method and symbolism completes this original, beautiful and exceedingly moving book."
                                                                        Anne Stevenson

The Plenitude We Cry For

COVER DESIGN BY FRANCES J. ELFENBEIN   0-385-05646-X PAPERBOUND